CROWN FINANCIAL MINISTRIES

Biblical Financial Study

LEADER'S GUIDE

PO Box 100
Gainesville GA 30503-0100
(800) 722-1976 / www.crown.org

TABLE OF CONTENTS

WEB SITE

CROWN has designed a web site as a resource to provide students and leaders with up-to-date and detailed financial information. It contains the forms used in this study, helpful articles, a categorized list of the verses dealing with possessions, links to other useful web sites, and much more.

Visit the web site at **www.crown.org** for a world of information.

MISSION STATEMENT

*Teaching people God's financial principles
in order to know Christ more intimately
and to be free to serve Him.*

COURSE OBJECTIVES/LEADER'S RESPONSIBILITIES

OBJECTIVES OF THE STUDY

1. Encourage people to experience more intimate fellowship with Christ.

Luke 16:11 expresses the correlation between how we handle our resources and the quality of our fellowship with the Lord: *"If therefore you have not been faithful in the use of worldly wealth, who will entrust the true riches to you?"*

2. Challenge each person to invite Jesus Christ to be their Lord.

We believe money is the primary competitor with Christ for the lordship of our lives. Jesus said, *"No man can serve two masters, you will love one and hate the other . . . you cannot serve God and Mammon* [money]*"* (Matthew 6:24).

3. Build close relationships among the participants.

4. Help students put their financial house in order.

THE PRIMARY RESPONSIBILITIES OF THE LEADER

1. Unconditionally love and encourage your students.

People are more receptive to spiritual truth when they have been loved. People want to know how much you care before they care how much you know.

2. Hold your students accountable.

3. Be a model of faithfulness.

Luke 6:40 reads, *"Everyone, after he has been fully trained, will be like his teacher."* Leaders must be faithful to always arrive early, pray consistently for your students, know the memory verses fluently, and have your homework and practical applications prepared.

4. Conform to the CROWN FINANCIAL MINISTRIES' procedure of leading the study.

1. The Leader's Guide

The *Leader's Guide* is divided into three sections:

- Information the leader needs to know
- The weekly homework guides
- The prayer logs, care log, and student evaluation

2. Practical Application Video

Each week toward the end of class you will play a segment of the *Practical Application Video*. There are 12 segments of the video—one for each week of the study. For example, at the end of Week 4, play segment 4 of the video.

The *Practical Application Video* explains the next week's assignment and communicates other important information the students need to know. After viewing the video take time to answer any questions the students may have. Each small group should have a copy of the *Practical Application Video*.

3. Group Size

There should be two leaders in each group.

The maximum number of students in a group varies depending upon how many students are married couples and how many are individuals. Under no circumstance should there be more than **eight** students. We limit the size of the group because the group dynamic is damaged if the group is too large. The table below will assist you in determining your group size.

Leaders:	Couple	Couple/Single	Couple/Single	Couple/Single	Single
Co-leaders:	Couple	Couple/Single	Couple/Single	Couple/Single	Single
Students:	Couple	Couple	Couple	Couple	Single
	Couple	Couple	Couple	Single	Single
	Couple	Couple	Single	Single	Single
	Couple	Single	Single	Single	Single
		Single	Single	Single	Single
Totals:	4 Leaders 8 Students	2-4 Leaders 8 Students	2-4 Leaders 7 Students	2-4 Leaders 6 Students	2 Leaders 5 Students

4. Meeting Time

The groups meet for two hours once each week for twelve weeks. The time and day the group meets should be the one most convenient for the participants. Groups may meet anywhere—in homes, offices or churches. There are couples, men-only, women-only, and mixed groups.

5. Promoting Financial Products and Services

No one may use their affiliation with CROWN FINANCIAL MINISTRIES to promote or influence the sale of any investments or financial services or professional services.

6. Student Evaluation Sheet

The Student Evaluation Sheet is found on page 87 and should be used by the leader to record the performance of the students after each class.

7. Certificate of Achievement

The leaders should award the Certificate of Achievement to those students who have been faithful. Five certificates are inserted in the *Leader's Guide*.

8. Scheduling the Study

The study is usually conducted three times each year, starting mid-January, the first part of May, and mid-September. However, you may begin a CROWN group anytime.

9. More About CROWN FINANCIAL MINISTRIES

What is CROWN FINANCIAL MINISTRIES? CROWN is an interdenominational ministry that has developed a comprehensive program to train people of all ages to apply the financial principles from the Bible.

Why is the ministry named CROWN? The reason this ministry is named CROWN is to remind us to always honor the Lord and serve people:

- CROWN FINANCIAL MINISTRIES exists to glorify Jesus Christ. He wore a Crown of Thorns when, out of unfathomable love, He died for us (John 19:1-5). Just as the 24 elders in Revelation 4:9-11 cast their crowns before the throne of God, so those serving with CROWN should honor Christ in all that we do.
- CROWN FINANCIAL MINISTRIES exists to serve people. Paul wrote to the Philippians, "*Therefore, my beloved brothers whom I long to see, my joy and crown*" (Philippians 4:1).

Financial Information: CROWN FINANCIAL MINISTRIES is a non-profit, tax-exempt organization governed by a Board of Directors, none of whom receive a salary from serving on the Board. Book royalties are the property of the ministry. CROWN is a member of the Evangelical Council for Financial Accountability, whose members must adhere to certain standards, including an annual audit. The ministry is funded primarily by donations, the bulk of which come from graduates of CROWN studies, radio listeners, or churches that are implementing CROWN.

As the group is being assembled, the leaders should diligently **pray** that the Lord will bring just the right students into the group. Then the leaders should meet with their students as a group at least **two weeks** before the study begins. This Student Orientation may be done just with the members of your small group or there may be a church-wide or city-wide orientation.

1. Start to love the students and build relationships.

2. Review the students' requirements by viewing the Student Orientation video.

The CD-ROM in the back of this *Leader's Guide* contains this video.

The requirements are designed to take approximately two hours each week outside of class. If for any reason someone comes to the class unprepared, they will not be allowed to participate in the discussion. The student requirements are:

- Daily homework
- Scripture to memorize each week
- Weekly practical application
- Daily prayer for each participant
- Attend ten of the twelve classes

3. The other important "ground rules."

- The class opens and closes in prayer
- Scriptures are memorized in the version used in the CROWN materials and not in another version of the Bible
- The classes start and stop precisely on time
- Group discussions are strictly confidential
- Students are trained to be future leaders by each person leading one of the weekly meetings
- No one will be embarrassed by being required to expose their financial situation

4. Dispense the materials and collect payment.

One student set is required for each person or married couple. A student set for couples contains two *Student Manuals*. A student set for an individual contains one *Student Manual*. Collect payment for the class.

5. The Personal Information Sheet

Ask each student to complete the Personal Information Sheet found on page 5 in the *Practical Application Workbook* and send it to CROWN. The Personal Information Sheets may be completed and transmitted over the web by visiting www.crown.org/piform.asp.

6. Assign the Week 1 homework

The assignment is found on page 8 of the *Student Manual* and must be completed prior to attending Week 1. The assignment is to read *Your Money Counts*, memorize Luke 16:11, and answer the homework questions. Ask the students to bring their calendar to the first class to schedule the two socials.

PRAYER LOG

To help the participants develop a more consistent prayer life, we utilize the prayer log. During the first meeting, ask each person or couple to provide the small group information at the top of the prayer log—their name, phone number, etc.

- One prayer log should be filled out for each person or couple.
- End each class by taking prayer requests from each member or couple. The requests need not be limited to financial concerns. Prior to taking a request, inquire if they have experienced any answers to their prayer requests. There may be more than one request per week.
- To save time, ask the participants to complete their own prayer log before coming to class. Each member is required to pray daily for every member in the group during the twelve weeks. Examine the sample prayer log below.

"Pray for one another." — JAMES 5:16

Name **Don Norman**   Spouse **Janet**

Home phone **321-2525**   Children (ages) **Matthew (12)**

Buisness phone **542-1378**   **Danielle (6)**

E-mail **djnorman@wayout.net**

Home address **272 Nelsen Ave.**
Little Rock, AR 72212

WEEK	PRAYER REQUEST(S)	ANSWERS TO PRAYER
1	Matthew's cold to get better Don's relationship with boss improve	
2	Don's relationship with boss improve Janet's neighbor come to know Christ	Matthew is completely well
3	Our family faithful in applying God's financial principles	Don's relationship with his boss has improved
4	Our family to get out of debt Danielle to have good time at school	
5		

1. Love your students outside of class

Care log. The purpose of the Care Log is to insure that the leaders contact their students each week to encourage and love them. The weekly contacts may be by telephone, mail, e-mail, or in person. The two leaders should alternate each week in their responsibility to contact the students by deciding who will contact students on the odd numbered weeks and who will contact the students on the even numbered weeks.

The students should not be aware of the Care Log. The leaders should inspect each other's Care Log weekly to encourage faithfulness.

CARE LOG

Leaders: **John Cole and Tim Manor**

Beginning Date of Small Group Study: **January 12, 2001**

WEEK	Initials of leader responsible for contact	Student(s) B. Hunt	Student(s) Mr. T Turner Mrs. B Turner	Student(s) J. Morgan	Student(s) G. Jones	Student(s)	Student(s)
1	JC	Phone 1/13	Lunch 1/14	Phone 1/14	Postcard 1/15		
2	TM	Phone 1/20	Phone 1/21	Wrote 1/20	Saw in person		
3	JC						
4	TM						

Socials. The leaders should organize two social events for the students. These activities may be for a dessert, a meal, or any other relaxed setting that will encourage the development of relationships. The first social should be scheduled mid-way through the study. The second social should be held as soon as possible after the study. It is also a good idea to visit the students where they work or live.

2. Love your students inside of class

The leader's attitude should be loving, humble, and caring—not a critical or a "know-it-all" attitude. We are students-among-students, in that we all are growing in understanding the unfathomable Word of God.

After a student answers a question, encourage, affirm, and thank them. If an answer is incorrect, be careful not to discourage the student by responding harshly or negatively. Maintain good eye contact and be attentive because we communicate through our body language.

HOW TO SELECT AND TRAIN LEADERS FROM AMONG YOUR STUDENTS

1. Set the Stage

In the student orientation tell your students that you are going to train them to be leaders. Whether they become leaders is dependent upon their desire to lead the study and their faithfulness during the study.

2. Test your Students

The most experienced leader should lead weeks one and two. The co-leader should lead weeks three and four. Then each student should be invited to lead one or two of the weeks.

3. Selection of Leaders

You should consider only those students who are faithful during the study.

4. Validation of Leaders

Any potential leader should be approved by the church leadership if the study is conducted within a church.

5. Invitation of Leaders

After a person has been selected and validated as a leader, invite them to lead the study. If they decide to become a leader, they need to be trained.

6. Training of Leaders

For your students to be qualified to lead the study, they should:

- Study the *Leader's Guide*.
- Complete a training session during which they view the *Leader's Training Video*. The CD-ROM in the back of this *Leader's Guide* contains this video. This training session may be conducted by a church. or in a city-wide event, or it may be self-study using the CD-ROM.

1. Open with prayer. We recommend that you pray on your knees.

2. Individually recite the Scripture to memorize.

3. Confirm that the Practical Applications have been completed.

4. Conduct the group discussion. The discussion should proceed as follows:

   - Different group members read the Scriptures for a particular day's homework.
   - Proceed in a circle asking every person to answer all the questions for that day's homework. If the answer to a question is obvious, it is not necessary for more than one person to answer the question.
   - In a couples group, everyone should answer the Day One Homework, then the men and women should alternate in answering the questions for Days Two through Six Homework.

5. Complete the items listed in the Remaining Agenda in consecutive order.

6. View the *Practical Application Video*.

7. Share prayer requests and write them in the Prayer Logs.

8. End in prayer.

SMALL GROUP DYNAMICS

- In Diagram 1 the sole focus is on the leader who does all the talking. The students are passive. This is not how CROWN is designed.
- Diagram 2 reflects a group interacting with one another, and a leader who guides and facilitates the discussion. The leader must establish an environment in which students have the freedom to express their insights and questions.

DIAGRAM 1
The Wrong Method

DIAGRAM 2
The Correct Method

LEADER

How to Begin Crown in the Church

An explanation of how to begin CROWN in a church is described in detail in the *Church Manual* and the *Church Training Video*. The following is an abbreviated outline of the steps:

1. **Introduce** CROWN FINANCIAL MINISTRIES **to the pastor/church leadership.**
   Meet with the pastor and appropriate church leadership to explain the study. The *Introducing Crown Financial Ministries to the Church Leadership* video is very helpful in describing the program. The CD-ROM in the back of this *Leader's Guide* contains this video. To successfully implement the study in a church, it is essential to have the active support of the church leadership.

2. **Select and train the small group leaders.**
   The number of people that will need to be trained is determined by the number of groups the church wants to begin.

3. **Select the students for the initial group or groups.**
   The major objectives of the initial groups are to multiply the number of people qualified to lead and to enable some of the church leadership to experience the study.

4. **Choose the church initial coordinator.**
   The church coordinator (usually a layperson) has the overall responsibility of implementing Crown Financial Ministries within the church. This position requires a commitment of time and effort and should be the person's primary, if not sole, ministry. The pastor should be involved in the selection process. The first person serving in this role is often gifted as an initiator, but will want to be replaced in a year or two.

5. **When** CROWN **is opened to the church.**
   - Bathe every presentation in prayer, asking the Lord to motivate the students He wants in the study.
   - Communicate the content and benefits of the study, and never use any "hard sell" tactics. Describe the requirements, accountability, and the need to invest two hours of preparation each week outside of class.
   - Churches have used several methods to present the study: A CROWN graduate's personal recommendation to a friend, the pastor's recommendation from the pulpit, an announcement in the church bulletin, and using the *Introducing Crown to Potential Small Group Students* video. The CD-ROM in the back of this *Leader's Guide* contains this video.

There are four elements a leader must put in place to build a successful small group study:

1. The leader must love the students.
2. The leader must hold the students accountable.
3. The leader must model faithfulness.
4. The leader must conduct the study according to the CROWN FINANCIAL MINISTRIES procedure.

We want to serve you and help you maintain a high standard of excellence. In order to assist you, an experienced CROWN small group leader may visit your group. After the class has ended and the students have departed, the experienced leader will meet with you to discuss the class and answer any questions. This is the checklist that will be used as a guide:

---

1. Describe how the leaders loved the students:

2. Did the leaders hold the students accountable to fulfill their responsibilities?

☐ Scripture Memory   ☐ Practical Application

☐ Homework   ☐ Daily Prayer

3. Did the leaders model faithfulness in the following areas?

☐ Scripture Memory   ☐ Practical Application

☐ Homework   ☐ Daily Prayer

☐ Student Evaluation Sheet   ☐ Care Log/Two Socials Scheduled

4. Did the leaders conduct the study according to the CROWN FINANCIAL MINISTRIES agenda?

☐ Start on Time   ☐ Correctly Lead Discussion

☐ Opening Prayer   ☐ View *Practical Application Video*

☐ Scripture Memory   ☐ Prayer Requests

☐ Confirm Practical Application   ☐ Ending Prayer / Stop on Time

Additional Comments:

If you have a desire to help others learn God's way of handling money, there are four places you can serve with CROWN as illustrated in the baseball diamond.

1. **As a small group leader or co-leader.** The heroes of CROWN FINANCIAL MINISTRIES are the leaders and co-leaders because the small group is where life-change takes place.
2. **As a Church Coordinator or on the Church Team.** If you want to impact your entire church, you may serve as the Church Coordinator or on the church team.
3. **As a City Director or on the City Team.** If you have a desire to influence your community, third base is for those who serve as a City Director or on the City Team. In order for CROWN to have a broad impact on a larger city or populated area, it is necessary to have a full-time City Director and a functioning team of volunteers.
4. **Beyond the City.** Home plate is for those who have a "missionary spirit" and wish to help introduce CROWN studies to other cities and even other countries. If you wish to serve your church, or your city, or even beyond your city, visit CROWN's Web site at www.crown.org/jobs.asp for more information on these positions.

THE NEXT STEP

1. **What I need to do to begin my first group.**

   ▪ My leader or co-leader is:

   ▪ My potential students are (Concentrate on selecting students who have the potential to become future small group leaders. It is also helpful to have someone representing the church leadership participate.):

   ▪ Describe how you will ask the students to participate:

   ▪ Describe how you will schedule the Student Orientation:

   ▪ My goal is to start my first group by this date:

2. **What I need to do to help Crown grow in my church.**

   ▪ Meet with my pastor/church leadership to discuss CROWN FINANCIAL MINISTRIES.

   ▪ The acting Crown Church Coordinator is:

   ▪ Those who will serve on the initial Church Team:

Leader's Guide for Week 1

INTRODUCTION

How We Handle Money Impacts Our Relationship With the Lord

THE MASTER REWARDS
HIS FAITHFUL SERVANTS—
*"Well done, good and faithful
servant . . . enter into the joy
of your master."*

Matthew 25:21

CROWN'S OVERVIEW OF WEEK 1: The primary objectives for week 1 are to begin to develop close relationships among the participants and reinforce the study requirements. Leaders should read the Introduction Notes prior to attending class.

NOTE: The blank space following each agenda number is for the leader to fill in the scheduled time for each agenda item. For example, if your class begins at 7:00, #1 would read 7:00, #2 would read 7:05, #3 would read 7:10, and so forth. This is designed to assist the leader in monitoring the time so that the class will end punctually.

AGENDA:

1. _____ (5 minutes) **Open in prayer.**

2. _____ (5 minutes) **Each person individually recites from memory *Luke 16:11*.**

   "If therefore you have not been faithful in the use of worldly wealth*, who will entrust the true riches to you?"

3. _____ (5 minutes) **If you have not done so before, collect the Personal Information Sheets found on page 5 in the *Practical Application Workbook* and review the requirements found on page 4 of the *Student Manual*.**

4. _____ (70 minutes) **Ask each person to introduce themselves, beginning with a leader. Ask them to share how they were introduced to Jesus Christ, what they do for a living, and something about their family. To determine how much time each person is allotted, divide the number of people into 70 minutes. The leaders should communicate this time constraint. If a student is too brief, the leader should gently ask additional questions to provide the student with an opportunity to express himself or herself more fully.**

5. _____ (10 minutes) **Begin the homework discussion.**

   * The words *worldly wealth* from the New International Version have been substituted for the words *unrighteous mammon* from the New American Standard Version to clarify the meaning of this passage.

1. What was the most helpful information you learned from reading *Your Money Counts*?

Read *Isaiah 55:8-9*

2. Based on this passage, do you think God's financial principles will differ from how most people handle money? What do you think would be the greatest difference?

> **NOTE TO LEADER:** Crown's comments, enclosed in brackets, will follow each question. Following CROWN'S comments there will be space for the leader's response to the question.

[**God's economy operates on entirely different principles. Most people do not believe the Lord plays a role in finances, but Scripture reveals He has the dominant role**].

Then read *Luke 16:11*.

3. What does this verse communicate to you about the importance of managing possessions faithfully?

[**How we handle money affects our fellowship with Christ.**]

4. How does handling money impact our fellowship with the Lord?

[**If we are unfaithful with money, our fellowship with the Lord will suffer.**]

Scripture memory helps: The memory verses are found in the back of the *Practical Application Workbook* and are designed to be removed and carried with you throughout the day. The verses have been set to music and are on the CD at the end of the *Practical Application Workbook*.

INTRODUCTION

REMAINING AGENDA:

1. _____ (5 minutes) **Play the Week 1 segment of the *Practical Application Video* which reviews what the students are required to do for next week.**

   - Read the Introduction Notes on pages 9 to 11 in the *Student Manual*.
   - Complete the God's Part Homework on pages 14 to 17 in the *Student Manual*.
   - Begin Recording Income and Spending and complete the Personal Financial Statement on pages 7 to 13 in the *Practical Application Workbook*.

2. _____ (5 minutes) **After viewing the Week 1 segment of the *Practical Application Video*, answer any questions the students have about next week's assignment.**

   - **REVIEW THE CALENDAR** to determine if any regularly scheduled classes fall on a holiday. If there are any conflicts, please reschedule at this meeting.
   - **SCHEDULE THE TWO SOCIALS.**
   - **COMPLETE THE PRAYER LOGS.** Participants should have one Prayer Log for each person or couple, including himself or herself.

3. _____ (10 minutes) **Take prayer requests and note them in the Prayer Log.**

4. _____ (5 minutes) **End in prayer.**

REMINDER FOR LEADERS: Complete the students' evaluations on page 87. Decide which leader will be responsible for what week on the Care Log. Be sure to contact each student this week. If you collect any Personal Information Sheets, please give them to the CROWN church or city leader or send them to CROWN FINANCIAL MINISTRIES.

GOD'S PART

Lord Is Owner of All

DAVID—
WORSHIPING THE LORD AT THE DEDICATION
OF THE OFFERING FOR THE TEMPLE

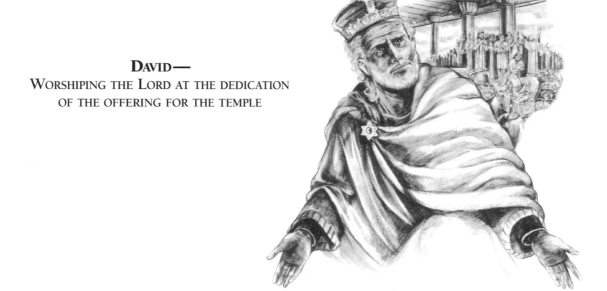

REMINDER FOR LEADERS: Complete the students' evaluations. Decide which leader will be responsible for what week on the Care Log. Be sure to contact each student this week. If you collect any Personal Information Sheets, please give them to the Crown church or city leader or send them to CROWN FINANCIAL MINISTRIES.

AGENDA:

1. _____ (5 minutes) **Open in prayer.**

2. _____ (5 minutes) **Each person individually recites from memory *1 Chronicles 29:11-12,* LB.**

   "Everything in the heavens and earth is yours, O Lord, and this is your kingdom. We adore you as being in control of everything. Riches and honor come from you alone, and you are the Ruler of all mankind; your hand controls power and might and it is at your discretion that men are made great and given strength."

3. _____ (5 minutes) **Confirm that everyone has completed the practical application of the Personal Financial Statement, has started the Recording Income and Spending worksheet, and made an appointment to secure a will or trust. Answer any questions concerning the practical applications.**

4. _____ (80 minutes) **Begin the group discussion.**

GOD'S PART

DAY ONE

1. Read the Introduction Notes on pages 9 to 11 and answer: What information especially interested you?

    LEADERS—The participants should read the Notes before class, not during the class.

    [Emphasize that how we handle money affects our fellowship with Christ.]

2. Comment on any personal challenges you felt after learning the three reasons the Bible says so much about money.

DAY TWO

Read *Deuteronomy 10:14; Psalm 24:1;* and *1 Corinthians 10:26.*

1. What do these passages teach about the ownership of your possessions?

    [The Lord owns everything in the world.]

Then read *Leviticus 25:23; Psalm 50:10-12;* and *Haggai 2:8.*

2. What are some of the specific items that the Lord owns?

    Leviticus 25:23 — [**God owns all the land.**]

    Psalm 50:10-12 — [**God owns all the animals.**]

    Haggai 2:8 — [**God owns all the gold and silver.**]

3. Prayerfully evaluate your attitude of ownership toward your possessions. Do you consistently recognize the true owner of those possessions? Give two practical suggestions to help recognize God's ownership.

[Alter your vocabulary by dropping the possessive pronouns ("my", "mine", and "ours") and substituting "His" or "the" instead. For thirty days, each morning and night, meditate and prayerfully recite *1 Chronicles 29:11-12.*]

    ■

    ■

DAY THREE

Read *1 Chronicles 29:11-12* and *Psalm 135:6.*

1. What do these verses say about the Lord's control of circumstances?
[**The Lord is in control of all circumstances.**]

Then read *Proverbs 21:1; Isaiah 40:21-24;* and *Acts 17:26.*

2. What do these passages tell you about the Lord's control of people?

Proverbs 21:1— [**God controls the heart of each person.**]

Isaiah 40:21-24— [**The Lord is in absolute control of all people.**]

Acts 17:26— [**The Lord controls the boundaries and duration of every nation.**]

3. Do you normally recognize the Lord's control of all events? If not, how can you become more consistent in recognizing His control?

LEADER—you should have approximately **one hour** of class time remaining. We recommend a three-minute stretch break for your group at this time.

DAY FOUR

Read *Genesis 45:4-8; Genesis 50:19-20;* and *Romans 8:28.*

1. Why is it important to realize that God controls and uses even difficult circumstances for good in the life a godly person?

[**God works every circumstance for good in the life of those who love Him and are yielded to Him as Lord. Joseph suffered difficult circumstances, but God orchestrated those difficulties for ultimate good.**]

2. How does this perspective impact you today?

3. Share a difficult circumstance you have experienced and how the Lord ultimately used it for good in your life.

Read *Psalm 34:9-10; Matthew 6:31-33;* and *Philippians 4:19.*

1. What has the Lord promised about meeting your needs?

   [God has promised to provide our needs if we seek first the kingdom of God and His righteousness.]

2. Give an example from the Bible of the Lord providing for someone's needs in a supernatural way.

   [Several of the many examples of God's provision: Israel in the wilderness (Exodus 16:4-35), Jesus feeding the five thousand (Matthew 14:15-21) and the four thousand (Matthew 15:32-38), and the Lord sending ravens to feed Elijah (1 Kings 17:4-6).]

3. How does this apply to you today?

   [The Lord continues to provide for us today.]

DAY SIX

Read *Job 1:20-22* and *Jeremiah 27:5.*

1. What do these verses communicate to you about how the Lord distributes material possessions?

   Job 1:20-22 — **[The Lord gives and takes away material possessions.]**

   Jeremiah 27:5 — **[The Lord gives material possessions to whomever He pleases.]**

GOD'S PART

Then read *Matthew 25:14-15*.

2. What does this passage tell us about how the Lord dispenses material possessions?
   [**The Lord dispenses material possessions unequally among His children.**]

3. How should this influence our perspective of those who have more or less than we do?

REMAINING AGENDA:

1. _____ (10 minutes) **Play the Week 2 segment of the *Practical Application Video* which reviews what the students are required to do for next week. Answer any questions concerning the practical application.**

   - Read the God's Part Notes on pages 18 to 23 in the *Student Manual*.
   - Complete the God's Part Homework on pages 26 to 29 in the *Student Manual*.
   - Complete the Deed and Financial Goals on pages 15 to 21 in the *Practical Application Workbook*.

2. _____ (10 minutes) **Note in the Prayer Log requests and answers to prayers.**

3. _____ (5 minutes) **End in prayer.**

REMINDER FOR LEADERS: Remember to be vulnerable with your own financial challenges. Contact each student this week and record the communication in the Care Log on page 88.

OUR PART
Faithfulness Required

ABRAHAM—

FAITHFUL EVEN WITH SMALL THINGS

"Abram said to the king of Sodom, I have sworn to the Lord. . . . that I will not take a thread or a sandal thong or anything that is yours."

Genesis 14:22-23

CROWN'S OVERVIEW OF WEEK 3: We have the responsibility to be faithful stewards of the possessions God entrusts to us knowing that the Lord will hold us accountable for how we handle them. The leader should read the Our Part Notes prior to attending class.

AGENDA:

1. _____ (5 minutes) **Open in prayer.**

2. _____ (5 minutes) **Each person individually recites from memory *1 Corinthians 4:2*, KJV.**

   "Moreover, it is required in stewards that a man be found faithful."

3. _____ (5 minutes) **Confirm that everyone has completed the Financial Goals and Deed in the *Practical Application Workbook*. Ask four people to witness each Deed. Answer any questions concerning the practical applications.**

4. _____ (80 minutes) **Begin the group discussion.**

DAY ONE

Read the God's Part Notes on pages 18 to 23 and answer:

1. Do you encounter difficulty in consistently recognizing the Lord's ownership of all you possess? If so, what contributes to this difficulty?

2. How can you work to be more consistent in recognizing His ownership?
   [Encourage the students to meditate on *1 Chronicles 29:11-12* for the next 30 days.]

3. What personal benefits do you anticipate from this consistency?

DAY TWO

Read *Genesis 1:26* and *Psalm 8:4-6*.

1. What do these verses say about the authority God gave people?
   [People were given authority over the Lord's possessions.]

Then read *1 Corinthians 4:2*.

2. According to this verse what is your requirement as a steward?
   [We are responsible to be faithful as stewards.]

3. How would you define a steward?

[**A steward is a manager of another's property.**]

DAY THREE

Read *Hebrews 4:13* and *Psalm 139:1-3* and answer:

1. Is the Lord aware of all your thoughts and actions?

[**Yes, the Lord knows all our thoughts and actions.**]

Then read *Romans 14:10-12*, and answer.

2. What will happen to each of us in the future?

[**We will stand before the judgment seat of God and give an account of our actions.**]

3. How should this impact the way you live and spend money?

[**Each of us is going to stand before the Lord and be held accountable for how we lived and managed the Lord's possessions. This should motivate us to handle money strictly according to the Word of God. Our life on earth is so short when compared with eternity, yet how we live our life on earth will influence how we live throughout eternity.**]

DAYS FOUR AND FIVE

Read the parable of the talents in *Matthew 25:14-30*.

What does the parable illustrate about:

1. Our authority as stewards *(Matthew 25:14)*?

   [**The Lord gives us authority as stewards over His possessions.**]

2. Our responsibilities?

   [**We are to be faithful with whatever the Lord gives us. We are expected to act by faith and not be lazy or inactive because of fear.**]

3. Differing material resources given to each of us *(Matthew 25:15)*?

   [**Differing amounts are given to His children according to their ability.**]

4. Our being accountable for our actions *(Matthew 25:19)*?

   [**We are going to be held accountable for how we manage possessions. This parable does not teach that a believer can lose his or her salvation if unfaithful in handling possessions.**]

5. What blessings did the master give to the faithful stewards *(Matthew 25:20-23)*?

   [**The reward was greater responsibility and entering into the joy of the master.**]

6. Other principles?

   [**The one who was given two talents received exactly the same reward as the one who was given five talents. Therefore, we are to be faithful whether we have much or little.**]

OUR PART

Read *Luke 16:1-2.*

1. Why did the master remove the steward from his position?

   [**The steward was removed because he squandered the master's possessions.**]

2. How do you think this principle is applicable today?

Then read *Luke 16:10.*

3. Describe the principle found in this verse.

   [**If a person is unfaithful in a little matter, he or she will be unfaithful in much, and vice versa.**]

4. How does this apply in your situation?

Then read *Luke 16:12.*

5. Are we required to be faithful with other people's possessions? What happens if we are not?

   [**Yes, if one is unfaithful with that which is another's, the Lord will not entrust him with possessions of his own.**]

6. How does this apply to you?

OUR PART

REMAINING AGENDA:

1. _____ (10 minutes) **Play the Week 3 segment of the *Practical Application Video* which reviews what the students are required to do for next week. Answer any questions concerning the practical applications.**

   - Read the Our Part Notes on pages 30 to 34 in the *Student Manual.*

   - Complete the Debt Homework on pages 36 to 38 in the *Student Manual.*

   - Complete the Debt List and Debt Repayment Schedule on pages 23 to 30 in the *Practical Application Workbook.*

2. _____ (10 minutes) **Note on the Prayer Log requests and answers to prayers. Encourage everyone to be faithful to pray for each other daily.**

3. _____ (5 minutes) **End in prayer.**

REMINDER FOR LEADERS: Remember to complete the weekly evaluation. This week, at the latest, schedule a social event for the group. Also, pray daily for everyone in your group. This is your most important task as a leader.

PLEASE REVIEW the mechanics of how to lead the group discussion on page 11 to confirm that you are conducting the discussion correctly.

DEBT
Debt is Slavery

A GODLY WOMAN FINDS HERSELF IN DEBT
*"My husband is dead . . . and the creditor has come
to take my two children to be his slaves. . . . "*

2 Kings 4:1

CROWN'S OVERVIEW OF WEEK 4: Debt is a struggle for many and is discouraged in Scripture. This week challenge the students to establish the goal of becoming debt free. The leader should read the Debt Notes prior to attending class.

AGENDA:

1. _____ (5 minutes) **Open in prayer.**

2. _____ (5 minutes) **Each person individually recites from memory *Proverbs 22:7*, LB.**

   "Just as the rich rule the poor, so the borrower is servant to the lender."

3. _____ (5 minutes) **Confirm that everyone has completed the practical applications of the Debt List and the Debt Repayment Schedule. Answer any questions concerning the practical applications.**

4. _____ (80 minutes) **Begin the group discussion.**

DAY ONE

Read the Our Part Notes on pages 30 to 34 and answer:

1. How have you observed the Lord using money to mold your character?

2. What strengths have been developed in your character?

3. What weaknesses in your character still need to be addressed?

DAY TWO

Read *Deuteronomy 15:4-6; Deuteronomy 28:1, 2, 12;* and *Deuteronomy 28:15, 43-45.*

1. According to these passages how was debt viewed in the Old Testament?
   [**Debt was considered a curse. Being free from debt (being a lender) was a blessing.**]

2. What was the cause of someone getting in debt (becoming a borrower) or getting out of debt (becoming a lender)?
   [**Disobedience led to debt and obedience led to getting out of debt (being a lender).**]

Read *Romans 13:8; Proverbs 22:7;* and *1 Corinthians 7:23* and answer:

1. Is debt encouraged in Scripture? Why?

Romans 13:8 — [**We are encouraged to stay out of debt.**]

Proverbs 22:7 — [**The debtor is servant to the lender.**]

1 Corinthians 7:23 — [**We are instructed not to be slaves of men. Therefore, make every effort to get out and stay out of debt. To summarize: the Bible does not say that debt is sin, but it discourages indebtedness.**]

2. How does this apply to you personally and to your business?

3. Do you have a strategy to get out of debt? If you have a plan, please describe it.

DAY FOUR

Read *Psalm 37:21* **and** *Proverbs 3:27-28.*

1. What do these verses say about debt repayment?

    Psalm 37:21— [**A person who borrows but does not repay debts is called "wicked."**]

    Proverbs 3:27-28— [**Pay debts promptly if you have the resources. Many are taught to delay repayment to use other people's money as long as possible, but this is not biblical.**]

2. How will you implement this?

DAY FIVE

Read *2 Kings 4:1-7.*

1. What principles of getting out of debt can you identify from this passage?

[**We should seek the counsel of godly people, as well as the Lord's help and direction. His supernatural intervention is required whether He answers quickly, as in the case of the widow, or more slowly over time. We should use whatever resources are available—however small—in an effort to get out of debt. Involve the entire family in your effort to get out of debt.**]

2. Can you apply any of these principles to your present situation? How?

Read *Proverbs 22:26-27* and *Proverbs 17:18* and answer:

1. What does the Bible say about cosigning (striking hands, surety)?

> *Proverbs 22:26-27*— [**Do not cosign. It may cause you to lose assets you need.**]

> *Proverbs 17:18*— [**It is poor judgment to cosign.**]

Then read *Proverbs 6:1-5.*

2. If someone has cosigned, what should he or she attempt to do?

[**If we have cosigned, we are to humbly and diligently seek the release of our obligation.**]

REMAINING AGENDA:

1. _____ (10 minutes) **Play the Week 4 segment of the *Practical Application Video* which reviews what the students are required to do for next week. Answer any questions concerning the practical applications.**

   - Read the Debt Notes on pages 39 to 50 in the *Student Manual*.
   - Complete the Counsel Homework on pages 52 to 55 in the *Student Manual*.
   - Complete the Estimated Budget on pages 31 to 37 in the *Practical Application Workbook*.

2. _____ (10 minutes) **Note in the Prayer Logs requests and answers to prayer.**

3. _____ (5 minutes) **End in prayer.**

REMINDER FOR LEADERS: In order to more consistently recognize God's ownership, encourage your students to continue meditating on *1 Chronicles 29:11-12*. Contact each student this week and note this in the Care Log. Remind the students to visit Crown's web site at **www.crown.org** for more practical assistance in getting out of debt.

Leader's Guide for Week 5
COUNSEL
A Wise Person Seeks Advice

SOLOMON—
SOUGHT WISDOM FROM A MULTITUDE
OF COUNSELORS

CROWN'S OVERVIEW OF WEEK 5: Everyone should seek counsel when they need to make a major financial decision. In our culture people are discouraged from seeking counsel. The leader should read the Counsel Notes prior to attending class.

AGENDA:

1. _____ (5 minutes) **Open in prayer.**

2. _____ (5 minutes) **Each person individually recites from memory *Proverbs 12:15.***

   "The way of a fool is right in his own eyes, but a wise man is he who listens to counsel."

3. _____ (5 minutes) **Confirm that everyone has completed the practical application of the Estimated Budget. Answer any questions concerning the practical applications.**

4. _____ (80 minutes) **Begin the group discussion.**

DAY ONE

Read the Debt Notes on pages 39 to 50 and answer:

1. Are you in debt? If so, what steps do you sense the Lord wants you to take to become free of debt?

    [Encourage your students to work toward getting out of debt.]

2. What did you learn about debt that proved to be especially helpful?

DAY TWO

Read *Proverbs 12:15*; *Proverbs 13:10*; and *Proverbs 15:22* and answer:

1. What are some of the benefits of seeking counsel?

    Proverbs 12:15 — **[The person who listens to counsel is wise.]**

    Proverbs 13:10 — **[Wisdom comes to those who seek counsel, but the consequence of not seeking counsel is strife.]**

    Proverbs 15:22 — **[Plans succeed with counsel but fail without it.]**

2. What are some of the benefits you have experienced from seeking counsel?

3. What hinders you from seeking counsel?

Read *Psalm 16:7* and *Psalm 32:8* and answer:

1. Does the Lord actively counsel His children? [**The Lord does counsel His children.**]

Then read *Joshua 9:14-20* and *Psalm 106:13-15*.

2. What were the consequences of not seeking the Lord's counsel in these two passages?

> *Joshua 9:14-20*— [**Because the leaders did not seek the counsel of the Lord, they entered into a treaty that permitted foreigners to live in the Promised Land. This ultimately influenced Israel to worship foreign gods. Sometimes "facts" can be deceptive or change rapidly. Only the Lord accurately knows the future. We need to seek His direction and counsel when faced with a major decision.**]

> *Psalm 106:13-15*— [**A "wasting disease" was sent because they did not seek the counsel of the Lord.**]

3. Have you ever suffered for not seeking the Lord's counsel? If so, describe what happened.

4. How do you seek the Lord's counsel?
   [**We seek the counsel of the Lord primarily through prayer, the Bible, and godly people.**]

LEADER— you should have approximately **one hour** of class time remaining. We recommend a three-minute stretch break for your group at this time.

COUNSEL

Read *Psalm 119:24; Psalm 119:105; 2 Timothy 3:16-17;* and *Hebrews 4:12.*

1. Should the Bible also serve as your counselor? Why?
   [**We must seek the counsel of the Word of God because it gives direction for our lives.**]

Then read *Psalm 119:98-100.*

2. Living by the counsel of Scripture—

   ■ Makes us wiser than: [**Our enemies**]

   ■ Gives us more insight than: [**Our teachers**]

   ■ Gives us more understanding than: [**Those older and more experienced**]

3. Do you consistently read and study the Bible? If not, what prevents your consistency?

DAY FIVE

Read *Proverbs 1:8-9.*

1. Who should be among your counselors?
   [**Our parents should be among our counselors.**]

2. In your opinion, who should be the number-one human counselor of a husband? Of a wife? Why?
   [**The husband and wife are each other's most important human counselor.**]

Read *Proverbs 11:14* **and** *Ecclesiastes 4:9-12.*

3. What do these verses communicate to you?

    Proverbs 11:14— **[People fail without counsel, but many counselors lead to victory.]**

    Ecclesiastes 4:9-12—**[Two or three people working together are more productive than a single individual.]**

4. How do you propose to apply this principle in your personal and/or business life?

DAY SIX

Read *Psalm 1:1-3* **and answer:**

1. Who should you avoid as a counselor?
    [Avoid the wicked as your counselor.]

2. What is your definition of a wicked person?
    [A wicked person is one who lives his or her life without regard to God.]

Then read *Proverbs 12:5.*

3. Why should you avoid their counsel?
    [The thoughts of the wicked are not controlled by the Holy Spirit and are deceitful.]

4. Is there ever a circumstance in which you should seek the input of a person who does not know Christ? If so, when?

[**In our opinion, it is permissible to seek input from those who do not know Christ when you are gathering facts. After collecting the facts, solicit counsel from godly people before arriving at your decision.**]

REMAINING AGENDA:

1. _____ (10 minutes) **Play the Week 5 segment of the *Practical Application Video* which reviews what the students are required to do for next week. Answer any questions concerning the practical applications.**

   - Read the Counsel Notes on pages 56 to 63 in the *Student Manual*.
   - Complete the Honesty Homework on pages 66 to 70 in the *Student Manual*.
   - Complete Adjusting Your Budget on pages 39 to 44 in the *Practical Application Workbook*.

2. _____ (10 minutes) **Note in the Prayer Logs requests and answers to prayer.**

3. _____ (5 minutes) **End in prayer.**

REMINDER FOR LEADERS: Remember to complete the students' evaluations.

Leader's Guide for Week 6
HONESTY

DANIEL WAS HONEST
"They could find no ground of accusation or evidence of corruption, inasmuch as he was faithful, and no negligence or corruption was to be found in him" (Daniel 6:4).

CROWN'S OVERVIEW OF WEEK 6: Dishonest practices are common, but the Lord demands that His children act with absolute honesty and integrity. This section is one of the most challenging of the entire study. The leader should read the Honesty Notes prior to attending class.

AGENDA:

1. _____ (5 minutes) **Open in prayer.**

2. _____ (5 minutes) **Each person individually recites from memory *Leviticus 19:11*.**

   "You shall not steal, nor deal falsely, nor lie to one another."

3. _____ (5 minutes) **Confirm that everyone has completed the Adjusting Your Budget practical application. Answer any questions concerning the practical applications.**

4. _____ (80 minutes) **Begin the group discussion.**

DAY ONE

Read the Counsel Notes on page 56 to 63 and answer:

1. What elements of God's perspective of counsel especially interested you?

    [**Encourage married couples to seek counsel from their spouses.**]

2. Do you actively seek counsel when faced with a major financial decision? If not, how do you propose to do so in the future?

DAY TWO

Read *Leviticus 19:11-13; Deuteronomy 25:13-16; Ephesians 4:25;* **and** *1 Peter 1:15-16.*

1. What do these verses communicate to you about God's demand for honesty?

    Leviticus 19:11-13 — [**The Lord commands us to be honest.**]

    Deuteronomy 25:13-16 — [**The Lord demands honesty in our business dealings.**]

    Ephesians 4:25 — [**We are not to lie to one another.**]

    1 Peter 1:15-16 — [**We are to be holy in our behavior just as the Lord is holy.**]

2. Are you consistently honest in even the smallest details? If not, what will you do to change?

3. What are two factors that motivate or influence us to act dishonestly?

[**Some of the factors influencing dishonesty are greed, fearing that God will not provide for us, financial difficulties, and peer pressure.**]

- ■

- ■

4. How does this apply to you?

DAY THREE

Read *Exodus 18:21-22* and answer:

1. Does the Lord require honesty for leaders? Why?

[**The Lord requires leaders to be honest. A major criteria for selecting leadership was honesty, because a leader will influence either for good or evil those under his or her authority.**]

Then read **Proverbs 28:16** and *Proverbs 29:12*.

2. What are the consequences of dishonesty for people in leadership?

Proverbs 28:16 — [**A dishonest person will be removed from leadership.**]

Proverbs 29:12 — [**Subordinates will become dishonest.**]

3. How does this apply to you?

HONESTY

DAY FOUR

Read *Proverbs 14:2* and answer:

1. Can you practice dishonesty and still love God? Why?

   [**No, those who practice dishonesty hate the Lord. When a person is dishonest, he has concluded that God is not able to provide exactly what he needs, is incapable of discovering his dishonesty, and is powerless to discipline him. In short, the dishonest person acts as if the Lord does not exist.**]

Then read *Proverbs 26:28* and *Romans 13:9-10*.

2. According to these passages, can you practice dishonesty and still love your neighbor? Why?

   [**No, because a dishonest person hates those whom he hurts. However, love does no wrong to a neighbor. Because dishonesty always affects people, we cannot love and be dishonest at the same time.**]

DAY FIVE

Read *Psalm 15:1-5; Proverbs 12:22; Proverbs 20:7;* and *Isaiah 33:15-16* and answer:

1. What are some of the benefits of honesty?

   Psalm 15:1-5 — [**More intimate fellowship with the Lord.**]

   Proverbs 12:22 — [**An honest person is a delight to the Lord.**]

   Proverbs 20:7 — [**The children of an honest person are blessed.**]

   Isaiah 33:15-16 — [**The Lord will protect and provide for the needs of the honest.**]

Then read *Proverbs 3:32; Proverbs 13:11;* and *Proverbs 21:6.*

2. What are some of the curses of dishonesty?

    Proverbs 3:32 — [**A dishonest person is an abomination to the Lord.**]

    Proverbs 13:11 — [**Anything obtained dishonestly will be taken away.**]

    Proverbs 21:6 — [**Obtaining wealth by lying produces only temporary gains and eventually leads to death.**]

DAY SIX

Read *Exodus 22:1-4; Numbers 5:5-8;* and *Luke 19:8* and answer:

1. What does the Bible say about restitution?

[**Restitution was required under the Old Testament law. Zaccheus is an example of a person fulfilling this obligation. Restitution involved the return of the item acquired dishonestly plus a penalty.**]

2. If you have acquired anything dishonestly, how will you make restitution?

[**Ask forgiveness from the Lord, confess your dishonesty to the one who was harmed and make restitution. Sometimes restitution is a delicate and complex issue. The question of how to fulfill the principle of restitution should be prayerfully answered.**]

Then read *Exodus 23:8; Proverbs 15:27;* and *Proverbs 29:4.*

3. What is the biblical position on bribes?

[**You must never take a bribe, because it will influence your judgment. The person who is not involved with bribes will live, but a leader who takes bribes will be overthrown.**]

4. Have you ever been asked to give or take a bribe? If so, describe what happened.

REMAINING AGENDA:

1. _____ (10 minutes) **Play the Week 6 segment of the *Practical Application Video* which reviews what the students are required to do for next week. Answer any questions concerning the practical applications.**

   - Read the Honesty Notes on pages 71 to 80 in the *Student Manual.*
   - Complete the Giving Homework on pages 82 to 85 in the *Student Manual.*
   - Complete Beginning Your Budget on pages 45 to 83 in the *Practical Application Workbook.*

2. **Ask students to recommend and/or contact people who might be future students. Forward any recommendations to the CROWN church or city leader.**

3. _____ (10 minutes) **Note in the Prayer Log requests and answers to prayers.**

4. _____ (5 minutes) **End in prayer.**

REMINDER FOR LEADERS: Encourage those who do not yet have a current will to secure one.

GIVING
Giving is Blessed

JESUS COMMENDS SACRIFICAL GIVING—
"A poor widow came in and put in two small copper coins which amount to a cent. And calling His disciples to Him, He said to them, 'This poor widow put in more than all the contributors to the treasury; for they all put in out of their surplus, but she, out of her poverty, put in all she owned, all she had to live on.'"

Mark 12:42-44

CROWN'S OVERVIEW OF WEEK 7: Communicate the importance of giving with the proper attitude. The leaders should read the Giving Notes prior to attending class.

AGENDA:

1. _____ (5 minutes) **Open in prayer.**

2. _____ (5 minutes) **Each individual recites from memory *Acts 20:35*.**

   "Remember the words of the Lord Jesus, that He Himself said, 'It is more blessed to give than to receive'" .

3. _____ (5 minutes) **Confirm that everyone has completed the Beginning Your Budget practical application, and check their progress in procuring a will. Answer any questions concerning the practical applications.**

4. _____ (80 minutes) **Begin the group discussion.**

GIVING

DAY ONE

Read the Honesty Notes on pages 71 to 80 and answer:

1. How does the example of Abraham in *Genesis 14:21-23* challenge you to be honest?

   [**Abraham made a commitment to the Lord not to take even a thread or a sandal thong. We need to make a similar commitment to be honest in even the smallest matters.**]

2. Ask the Lord to reveal any areas of dishonesty in your life. How do you propose to deal with these areas?

DAY TWO

Read *Matthew 23:23*; *1 Corinthians 13:3*; and *2 Corinthians 9:7* and answer:

1. What do each of these passages communicate about the importance of the proper attitude in giving?

   Matthew 23:23 — [**The Pharisees gave precisely the correct amount—a tithe of even their mint leaves. But because they gave with the wrong heart attitude, the Lord rebuked them.**]

   1 Corinthians 13:3 — [**Giving without a heart of love is of no value to the giver.**]

   2 Corinthians 9:7 — [**Do not give grudgingly or under compulsion, but rather give cheerfully. The proper attitude is crucial.**]

2. How do you think a person can develop the proper attitude in giving?

   [**The proper attitude is the key issue in the area of giving. The only way to give out of a heart of love is to consciously give each gift to Jesus Christ Himself as an act of worship.**]

3. After prayerfully evaluating your attitude in giving, how would you describe it?

DAY THREE

Read *Acts 20:35* **and answer:**

1. How does this principle from God's economy differ from the way most people view giving?

   [**In the Lord's economic system it is more blessed to give than to receive. Most people believe the opposite.**]

2. List the benefits for the giver, which are found in each of the following passages:

   Proverbs 11:24-25 — [**There is a material increase—in the Lord's time and way—to the giver.**]

   Matthew 6:20 — [**We can lay up treasures in heaven which we will be able to enjoy throughout all eternity.**]

   Luke 12:34 — [**The heart of the giver is drawn to Christ as treasures are given to Him.**]

   1 Timothy 6:18-19 — [**We can store treasures in heaven and "take hold of that which is life indeed."**]

LEADER—you should have approximately **one hour** of class time remaining. We recommend a three-minute stretch break for your group at this time.

DAY FOUR

Read *Genesis 14:20* **and answer:**

1. How much did Abraham give? Was his gift prior to the Old Testament Law?

   [**Abraham gave ten percent, a tithe, prior to the institution of the Law.**]

GIVING

Then read *Malachi 3:8-10.*

2. Was the tithe required under Old Testament Law?

[**The tithe was required under the law, and it was considered robbing God not to give these required gifts.**]

Then read *2 Corinthians 8:1-5.*

3. Identify three principles from this passage that should influence how much you give.

[**They first gave themselves to the Lord, asking Him to direct their giving. In the same way we need to submit ourselves to the Lord when determining how much to give.**]

[**They were so yielded to the Lord that despite difficult circumstances they begged to give.**]

[**They experienced tremendous joy as a result of their sacrificial giving**]

■

■

■

Prayerfully (with your spouse if you are married) seek the Lord's guidance to determine how much you should give. You will not be asked to disclose the amount.

DAY FIVE

Read *Matthew 15:4-6* and *1 Timothy 5:8* and answer:

1. Does the Bible require us to take care of our family members? How does this apply to you?

[**Yes, children are obligated to take care of their elderly or widowed parents. Parents are required to care for their young children.**]

Then read *Numbers 18:8-10,24; Galatians 6:6*; and *1 Timothy 5:17-18*.

2. What do these verses tell you about financially supporting your church and those who teach the Scriptures?

Numbers 18:8-10,24— **[Godly people have always been required to participate in the maintenance of the ministry. The Old Testament believer was required to care for the place of worship and the Levites who served in the ministry.]**

Galatians 6:6— **[Those who are taught the Scriptures should financially support their teachers.]**

1 Timothy 5:17-18— **[God's New Testament instrument is the church, and we are to adequately support those who serve as pastors and teachers.]**

DAY SIX

Read *Isaiah 58:6-11* and *Ezekiel 16:49* and answer:

1. What do these verses say about giving to the poor?

Isaiah 58:6-11— **[When we give to the poor, the Lord will protect us, answer our prayers and bless us with His joy]**.

Ezekiel 16:49 — **[The primary sins of Sodom were pride and not caring for the poor—even though they had an abundance of material goods.]**

Then study *Matthew 25:35-45*.

2. How does Jesus Christ identify with the poor?

[Jesus identifies personally with the poor. When we give to the poor, we are giving to Christ Himself. When we do not give to the poor, we are not giving to Christ, and He is left hungry and naked.]

Then read *John 13:27-29* and *Galatians 2:9-10*.

3. What do these verses communicate to you about giving to the poor?

John 13:27-29— [**We are given a glimpse of the lifestyle of Jesus. The only options the disciples discussed concerning spending of money were the purchase of a basic necessity or a gift to the poor.**]

Galatians 2:9-10— [**The disciples also had a deep concern for the poor. After Paul's confirmation to minister to the Gentiles, the only counsel the disciples gave him was not to forget the poor. Think of the many issues they could have discussed. Yet, they only asked Paul to remember the poor.**]

4. Are you currently giving to the poor? If not, what is hindering you?

[**Encourage your students to ask the Lord to bring one poor person into their lives.**]

REMAINING AGENDA:

1. _____ (10 minutes) **Play the Week 7 segment of the *Practical Application Video* which reviews what the students are required to do for next week. Answer any questions concerning the practical applications.**

   ▪ Read the Giving Notes on pages 86 to 94 in the *Student Manual*.

   ▪ Complete the Work Homework on pages 96 to 100 in the *Student Manual*.

   ▪ Review the Checking Account and Budget Hints on page 85 to 88 in the *Practical Application Workbook*.

2. _____ (10 minutes) **Note in the Prayer Log requests and answers to prayers.**

3. _____ (5 minutes) **End in prayer.**

Leader's Guide for Week 8

WORK
Work Diligently As Unto The Lord

NEHEMIAH WORKED HARD AND RELIED UPON THE LORD—

"And I also applied myself to the work on this wall . . . the wall was completed . . . this work had been accomplished with the help of our God."

Nehemiah 5:16, 6:15-16

CROWN'S OVERVIEW OF WEEK 8: Work can be one of the most fulfilling or frustrating areas of life. Our satisfaction is dependent on understanding the Lord's perspective of work. The leader should read the Work Notes prior to attending class.

AGENDA:

1. _____ (5 minutes) **Open in prayer.**

2. _____ (5 minutes) **Everyone individually recites from memory *Colossians 3:23-24.***

   "Whatever you do, do your work heartily, as for the Lord rather than for men; knowing that from the Lord you will receive the reward of the inheritance. It is the Lord Christ whom you serve."

3. _____ (5 minutes) **Confirm that everyone understands Your Checking Account practical application. Determine your students progress in securing a will. Answer any questions concerning the practical applications.**

4. _____ (80 minutes) **Begin the group discussion.**

NOTE: Please give your leader the name of anyone who would be interested in becoming a student in a future group.

DAY ONE

Read the Giving Notes on pages 86 to 94 and answer:

1. From God's perspective it is important to give with the proper attitude. How will this impact your giving?

   [We need to give each gift to the person of Jesus Christ out of a grateful heart filled with love, in order to be drawn more closely to the Lord and reap the other advantages intended for the giver.]

2. What truth about giving did you learn that proved especially stimulating? In what way?

DAY TWO

Read *Genesis 2:15.*

1. Why is it important to recognize that the Lord created work prior to sin entering the world?

   [Yes, work was instituted prior to sin entering the world. In the perfect, sinless environment of the Garden of Eden, God created work for our benefit. Work is not a result of sin and the curse.]

Then read *Genesis 3:17-19.*

2. What was the consequence of sin on work?

   [Work became difficult as a result of sin.]

WORK

Then read *Exodus 20:9* and *2 Thessalonians 3:10-12*.

3. What do these passages say to you about work?

    Exodus 20:9— [**Old Testament believers were required to work six days each week.**]

    2 Thessalonians 3:10-12— [**In the New Testament work is also required. This verse does not recommend hunger for those who cannot work because of physical or mental limitations; only those who are capable of working but choose not to work.**]

DAY THREE

Read *Genesis 39:2-5*; *Exodus 35:30-35*; *Exodus 36:1-2*; and *Psalm 75:6-7*.

1. What do each of these verses tell us about the Lord's involvement in our work?

    Genesis 39:2-5— [**The Lord is in control of success.**]

    Exodus 35:30-35— [**The Lord gives us job skills and the ability to teach.**]

    Exodus 36:1-2— [**The Lord gives us our skills and understanding.**]

    Psalm 75:6-7— [**The Lord controls promotion and demotion.**]

WORK

2. How do these truths differ from the way most people view work?

[**The biblical perspective of God's part in work is in remarkable contradiction to the culture around us that does not acknowledge the Lord in work.**]

3. How will this perspective impact your work?

[**Our work attitudes and actions should be dramatically different from those who do not recognize God's role in work. We should be humble in any of our accomplishments because God gives us skills, success, and promotion.**]

LEADER—you should have approximately **one hour** of class time remaining. We recommend a three-minute stretch break for your group at this time.

DAY FOUR

Read *Ephesians 6:5-9; Colossians 3:22-25;* and *1 Peter 2:18.*

1. What responsibilities do the employer and employee have according to these verses?

Employee responsibilities:

[**Sincere obedience to employer—even one who is not good and gentle; work as unto the Lord; work heartily.**]

Employer responsibilities:

[**The employer should serve and not threaten employees.**]

2. For whom do you really work? How will understanding this change your work performance?

[**We work for the Lord. This perspective will allow us to make a sincere effort—even in difficult circumstances—to serve those who are our superiors or subordinates.**]

WORK

Read *Proverbs 6:6-11; Proverbs 18:9;* and *2 Thessalonians 3:7-9* and answer:

1. What does the Lord say about working hard?

    Proverbs 6:6-11— **[Ants are commended for hard work and those who are lazy warned of poverty.]**

    Proverbs 18:9—**[A lazy person is compared to someone who destroys.]**

    2 Thessalonians 3:7-9—**[Paul modeled hard work.]**

2. Do you work hard? If not, describe what steps you will take to improve your work habits.

Then read *Exodus 34:21.*

3. What does this verse communicate to you about rest?
[Hard work should be balanced with adequate rest and tempered by other biblical priorities. Even during busy times, one day of rest each week was required.]

4. Do you get enough rest?

5. How do you guard against overwork?

WORK

Read *Proverbs 31:10-28* and *Titus 2:4-5.*

1. What do these passages tell us about women working?

   Proverbs 31:10-28— **[The excellent wife is diligent, works with her hands, acquires and prepares food; invests, provides clothes for the family, and sells merchandise. She works outside the home, but always with a focus toward the home.]**

   Titus 2:4-5— **[Young wives were encouraged to be workers at home.]**

2. If you are a woman, how does this apply to your situation?

Then read *2 Corinthians 6:14-18.*

3. How does this concept of "yoking" or "being bound together" apply to partnerships in business and work?

   [The principle of yoking applies to business partnerships. It is permissible for an employee to work for an employer who does not know Christ, but partnership with an unbeliever is discouraged.]

4. Can you give some examples from the Bible of people who retired?

   [Scripture gives no example of people retiring and gives only one direct refrence to retirement which is found in *Numbers 8:24-26*. The instruction there applied exclusively to the Levites who had worked on the tabernacle.]

WORK

5. Do you think retirement, as it is practiced in our culture, is biblically permissible? Why or why not?

[**Many people retire and cease all labor to pursue a life filled with leisure. This is not Biblical. We should seek to be productive as long as we are able.**]

REMAINING AGENDA:

1. _____ (10 minutes) **Play the Week 8 segment of the *Practical Application Video* which reviews what the students are required to do for next week. Answer any questions concerning the practical applications.**

   - Read the Work Notes on pages 101 to 111 in the *Student Manual*.

   - Complete the Investing Homework on pages 114 to 119 in the *Student Manual*.

   - Complete the Organizing Your Estate section on pages 89 to 93 of the *Practical Application Workbook*.

   Encourage your students to continue budgeting. Ask them to think of three creative ways to save money that would normally be spent. As the students share their ideas next week, this can be a powerful experience when they consider how steady savings grow over time.

2. _____ (10 minutes) **Note in the Prayer Logs requests and answers to prayers.**

3. _____ (5 minutes) **End in prayer.**

WORK

Leader's Guide for Week 9

INVESTING
CONSISTENTLY SAVE

JOSEPH —
GATHERED DURING THE 7 YEARS OF PLENTY
TO PROVIDE FOR THE 7 YEARS OF FAMINE

CROWN'S OVERVIEW OF WEEK 9: This week's objectives are to learn the proper biblical attitudes toward saving and investing and to teach the scriptural framework for savings and investing. **The leaders should not recommend any specific investments or financial products or services.** CROWN FINANCIAL MINISTRIES assumes no liability for any actions taken related to specific investments or savings. The leaders should read the Investing Notes prior to attending class.

AGENDA:

1. _____ (5 minutes) **Open in prayer.**

2. _____ (5 minutes) **Everyone individually recites from memory *Proverbs 21:20* and *Proverbs 21:5*.**

   "The wise man saves for the future, but the foolish man spends whatever he gets"
   (Proverbs 21:20, LB)

   and

   "Steady plodding brings prosperity; hasty speculation brings poverty"
   (Proverbs 21:5, LB).

3. _____ (5 minutes) **Confirm that everyone completed the Organizing Your Estate practical application, understands the Savings Goals and is continuing with their budget. Answer any questions concerning the practical applications.**

4. _____ (10 minutes) **Ask the students to share their creative ideas on how to save money that would normally be spent.**

5. _____ (70 minutes) **Begin the group discussion.**

I N V E S T I N G

Read the Work Notes on pages 101 to 111 and answer:

1. What in the notes proved especially stimulating or challenging? How will this impact you?

2. Do you usually recognize you are working for the Lord? If not, what can you do to be more aware that you work for the Lord?

DAY TWO

Read *Genesis 41:34-36; Proverbs 21:20;* and *Proverbs 30:24-25* and answer:

1. What do these passages communicate to you about savings?

   Genesis 41:34-36 — [**Joseph saved during a time of plenty to prepare for a coming famine.**]

   Proverbs 21:20 — [**Those who are wise save, but the foolish only consume.**]

   Proverbs 30:24-25 — [**Ants are commended as wise because they save.**]

2. If you are not yet saving, how do you propose to begin?

Read *Luke 12:16-21,34.*

3. Why did the Lord call the rich man a fool?
   [**The rich man was a fool because he stored up all his goods and was not rich toward God.**]

4. According to this parable, why do you think it is scripturally permissible to save only when you are also giving?

[If we save without giving, our hearts will be drawn to those possessions and away from Christ (v. 34).]

DAY THREE

Read *1 Timothy 5:8* and answer:

1. What is a scripturally acceptable goal for saving?

[It is permissible to save to meet the needs of our family.]

Then read *1 Timothy 6:9*.

2. What is a scripturally unacceptable reason for saving?

[It is wrong to desire to get rich. However, it is not wrong to become rich if it is a by-product of being a faithful steward.]

Then read *1 Timothy 6:10*.

3. According to this verse, why is it wrong to want to get rich (refer to *1 Timothy 6:9*)? Do you have the desire to get rich?

[When we want to get rich we are actually loving money. The desire to get rich is a common attitude that can destroy our fellowship with the Lord.]

Then read *1 Timothy 6:11*.

4. What should you do if you have the desire to get rich?

[You should flee from this desire and pursue godly living.]

INVESTING

DAY FOUR

Read *Proverbs 21:5; Proverbs 24:27; Proverbs 27:23-24; Ecclesiastes 3:1; Ecclesiastes 11:2;* and *Isaiah 48:17-18.*

1. What investment principle(s) can you learn from each of these verses, and how will you apply each principle to your life?

   Proverbs 21:5—[**Be a diligent, steady plodder, and not hasty in investing.**]

   Proverbs 24:27—[**Develop your means of producing an income before securing a house.**]

   Proverbs 27:23-24 — [**Know the status of your assets at all times.**]

   Ecclesiastes 3:1— [**Timing is important in investing.**]

   Ecclesiastes 11:2—[**Diversify your investments.**]

   Isaiah 48:17-18— [**The Lord teaches us to prosper, and we need to seek Him as we make investment decisions.**]

Read *Genesis 24:35-36; Proverbs 13:22;* and *2 Corinthians 12:14.*

1. Should parents attempt to leave a material inheritance to their children?

   [Yes, parents should try to leave a material inheritance to their children.]

2. How are you going to implement this principle?

Then read *Proverbs 20:21* and *Galatians 4:1-2.*

3. What caution should a parent exercise?

   Proverbs 20:21 — **[An inheritance should not be given into a child's care until the child is mature enough to manage the inheritance faithfully.]**

   Galatians 4:1-2 — **[The appointment of a guardian through a will or trust helps insure a child's maturity before receiving an inheritance.]**

DAY SIX

Gambling is defined as: playing games of chance for money, betting, taking great risks, and speculating. Some of today's most common forms of gambling are casino wagering, betting on sporting events, horse and dog races, and state-run lotteries.

1. What are some of the motivations that cause people to gamble?

   [People are motivated to gamble by the desire to get rich quick, greed, and by the prospect of getting something for nothing. Many want to become wealthy so they can quit working.]

2. Do these motives please the Lord? Why?

   [These motives do not please the Lord because they are contrary to His principles found in the Bible.]

INVESTING

Read *Proverbs 28:20* and *Proverbs 28:22*.

3. According to these passages, why do you think a godly person should not gamble (play lotteries, bet on sporting events, etc.)?

[A person who hastens after wealth is identified as evil and will experience poverty. Please encourage your students never to bet one penny. State lotteries are particularly enticing because they have been legalized by the government and glamorized by the media.]

4. How does gambling contradict the scriptural principles of working diligently and being a faithful steward of the Lord's possessions?

[Gambling is in direct opposition to the scriptural principles of diligent work and faithful stewardship. No productive work is required in gambling; thus, a person's character is not properly developed. The odds of winning are absurdly low, and a gambler is wasting the possessions the Lord has entrusted to him.]

REMAINING AGENDA:

1. _____ (10 minutes) **Play the Week 9 segment of the *Practical Application Video* which reviews what the students are required to do for next week. Answer any questions concerning the practical applications.**

   - Read the Investing Notes on pages 120 to 133 in the *Student Manual*.
   - Complete the Children Homework on pages 136 to 139 in the *Student Manual*.
   - Complete Organizing Your Insurance on pages 95 to 97 in the *Practical Application Workbook*.

2. _____ (10 minutes) **Note in the Prayer Log requests and answers to prayers.**

3. _____ (5 minutes) **End in prayer.**

REMINDER FOR LEADER: Please recommend the students who are qualified to be future leaders. Encourage those who do not yet have a current will to secure one. Remind the students to visit CROWN's web site at **www.crown.org** for much more practical information on investing.

Leader's Guide for Week 10

CHILDREN

Parents Are Responsible To Train Their Children To Be Faithful Stewards

CROWN'S OVERVIEW OF WEEK 10: I have yet to meet an adult whose parents lived the biblical financial principles and taught them systematically to their children. Consequently, children leave home ill-equipped to manage their financial future. The most effective way to train our children is for the parents to model biblical money management, and to have the children participate in this management using visual aids which they can understand. The leader should read the Children Notes prior to attending class.

AGENDA:

1. _____ (5 minutes) **Open in prayer.**

2. _____ (5 minutes) **Everyone individually recites from memory *Proverbs 22:6*.**

   "Train up a child in the way he should go, even when he is old he will not depart from it."

3. _____ (5 minutes) **Confirm that everyone has completed the Organizing Your Insurance practical application and is budgeting faithfully. Answer any questions concerning the practical applications.**

4. _____ (80 minutes) **Begin the group discussion.**

DAY ONE

Read the Investing Notes on pages 120 to 133 and answer:

1. What in the notes proved especially helpful?

2. Carefully study the principle of compounding in the Investing Notes. Assume you earned 10 percent interest and saved $1,000 a year. Approximately how much would you accumulate by age 65 if you started saving today?

   $_____ *(refer to the graph on page 127 in the Investing Notes).*

3. Describe the specific steps you intend to take to begin saving:

DAY TWO

Read *Deuteronomy 6:6-7; Deuteronomy 11:18-19; Proverbs 22:6; and Ephesians 6:4*.

1. According to these passages, who is responsible for teaching children how to handle money from a biblical perspective?

   [**It is the responsibility of the parents. Introduce the concept of establishing a strategy for independence—the goal of having each child independently managing their finances (with the exception of food and housing) by their senior year in high school.**]

2. Stop and reflect for a few minutes: Describe how well you were prepared to manage money when you first left home as a young person?

   [**Most children leave home ill-equipped to manage money.**]

NOTE: Answer the questions in **Day Three Homework** through **Day Six Homework** even if you have no children or they no longer live with you.

CHILDREN

DAY THREE

1. Describe how you propose to train your children to budget.

2. List four practical suggestions you will teach your children to become wise spenders.

    ▪

    ▪

    ▪

    ▪

LEADER—you should have approximately **one hour** of class time remaining. We recommend a three-minute stretch break for your group at this time.

DAY FOUR

1. Describe how you are going to teach your children how to save and invest.

    Save—

    Invest—

2. How are you going to train them to conform to the biblical principle of keeping out of debt?
   [Post a visual graph in a conspicuous place to chart your progress in getting out of debt.]

CHILDREN

DAY FIVE

1. What methods will you employ to train your children to be generous, cheerful givers?

[Children should see the results of their giving. For example, it is helpful if they give to a poor person they know or give to the church building fund where they can see the construction.]

DAY SIX

1. List four suggestions to teach your children to work hard and to work "as unto the Lord."

   ▪

   ▪

   ▪

   ▪

REMAINING AGENDA:

1. _____ (10 minutes) **Play the Week 10 segment of the *Practical Application Video* which reviews what the students are required to do for next week. Answer any questions concerning the practical applications.**

   ▪ Read the Children Notes on pages 140 to 147 in the *Student Manual*.

   ▪ Complete the Perspective Homework on pages 150 to 154 in the *Student Manual*.

   ▪ Complete Organizing Your Children on pages 99 to 103 in the *Practical Application Workbook*.

2. _____ (10 minutes) **Note in the Prayer Logs requests and answers to prayers.**

3. _____ (5 minutes) **End in prayer.**

REMINDER FOR LEADERS: Encourage your students to continue to budget.

INSTRUCT YOUR STUDENTS to complete the Involvement and Suggestions sheet found on page 109 in the *Practical Application Workbook*. The input from the students is very important for the continued improvement of this study. The students' Involvement and Suggestions sheet should be forwarded to Crown Financial Ministries. Send directly by visiting Crown's web site **www.crown.org/isform.asp** or by mail to PO Box 100, Gainesville GA 30503-0100.

CHILDREN

PERSPECTIVE

PAUL—
CONTENT IN EVERY CIRCUMSTANCE

CROWN'S OVERVIEW OF WEEK 11: This week we will determine our God-given standard of living. In many respects this section is the summary of the entire study. The leader should read the Perspective Notes prior to attending class.

AGENDA:

1. _____ (5 minutes) **Open in prayer.**

2. _____ (5 minutes) **Everyone individually recites from memory *Philippians 4:11-13.***

   "For I have learned to be content in whatever circumstances I am. I know how to get along with humble means, and I also know how to live in prosperity; in any and every circumstance I have learned the secret of being filled and going hungry, both of having abundance and suffering need. I can do all things through Him who strengthens me."

3. _____ (5 minutes) **Confirm that everyone has completed the Organizing Your Children practical application and is budgeting faithfully. Determine the progress of the students' effort to secure a will. Answer any questions concerning the practical applications.**

4. _____ (80 minutes) **Begin the group discussion.**

   Note: Think about your prayer request for the last class. It should be a "long-term" request the others can pray when they think of you.

DAY ONE

Read the Children Notes on pages 140 to 147 and answer:

What ideas from the notes will you incorporate in training children to be faithful stewards?

[Encourage your students to develop a "strategy for independence"—the goal of having each child managing their finances (with the exception of food and housing) by their senior year in high school.]

DAY TWO

Read *Genesis 13:5-11*; *Matthew 13:7; 22*, and *Matthew 19:16-23*.

Each passage contains a danger associated with riches. Identify the danger from each verse and share one insight that could significantly alter or impact your thinking.

Genesis 13:5-11— **[Wealth tends to separate people—even family members. The prospect of gaining wealth can lead to bad choices. Lot is an example. He chose to live in Sodom (a wicked city) because it was located in a prosperous setting.]**

Matthew 13:7, 22— **[Riches can destroy spiritual productivity.]**

Matthew 19:16-23— **[It is difficult for a rich person to enter the kingdom of God.]**

Significant insight:

DAY THREE

Read *Deuteronomy 30:15-16*; *Joshua 1:8*; and *Hebrews 11:36-40*.

1. What do each of these passages communicate to you about financial prosperity for the believer?

Deuteronomy 30:15-16 — **[One of the blessings of obedience was prosperity.]**

Joshua 1:8 — [**Knowing and obeying all of the commands in the Scriptures resulted in prosperity.**]

Hebrews 11:36-40 — [**Even godly people exercising faith have experienced poverty and difficult circumstances.**]

Reflect on the lives of Job, Joseph, David, and Paul.

2. Did these men ever experience periods of financial abundance and at other times a lack of financial prosperity?

[**Job, Joseph, David, and Paul each experienced periods of plenty and times of want.**]

3. Was their lack of financial prosperity a result of sin or lack of faith?

[**Their times of poverty usually were not a result of sin or lack of faith.**]

4. Should all Christians always prosper financially? Why?

[**Once a person has fulfilled all areas of being a faithful steward, he or she is in a position for the Lord to prosper him or her financially. However, the Lord may not for one of three reasons: (1) He is building our character (*Romans 5:3-4*); (2) He needs to discipline us in an area of our life where there is sin (*Hebrews 12:6, 10*); and (3) God's sovereignty (*Hebrews 11:36-40*).**]

Then read *Psalm 73:1-20*.

5. What does this passage tell you about the prosperity of the wicked?

[**The psalmist questioned why the wicked prospered. He was envious. Godliness did not seem to "pay off." Then the Lord revealed the wicked person's end—sudden, eternal punishment.**]

6. How does this impact your thinking?

DAY FOUR

Read *Luke 3:14; Philippians 4:11-13; and 1 Timothy 6:6-8.*

1. What do each of these passages communicate to you about contentment?

   Luke 3:14— [**Be content with your income.**]

   Philippians 4:11-13— [**Contentment is not something that occurs naturally; it is learned. We can learn to be content in any circumstance.**]

   1Timothy 6:6-8— [**Godliness with contentment is a means of great gain. We cannot take anything with us when we die, and we should be content with our basic needs satisfied.**]

2. How does our culture discourage contentment?

3. How do you propose to practice contentment?

DAY FIVE

Read *Matthew 22:17-21* and *Romans 13:1-7* and answer:

1. Does the Lord require us to pay taxes to the government? Why?

   [**The Lord requires us to pay taxes because He has instituted government to serve people. The consequence of tax evasion is punishment.**]

2. Do you think it is biblically permissible to reduce your taxes by using legal tax deductions? Why?

[**The government has authorized the use of legal tax deductions to reduce taxes and as an incentive for certain actions.**]

Read *James 2:1-9*.

3. What does Scripture say about partiality (showing favoritism)?

[**Do not show favoritism to the wealthy. It is sin to be partial.**]

4. Are you guilty of partiality based on a person's financial, educational, or social status?

Read *Romans 12:16* and *Philippians 2:3*.

5. How do you plan to overcome partiality?

[**Be of the same mind toward each person and consider each person as more important than yourself.**]

DAY SIX

Read *Mark 8:36-37*; *Acts 4:32-37*; and *1 Thessalonians 4:11-12*.

1. What do these passages communicate to you about lifestyle?

Mark 8:36-37— [**A person can become tremendously wealthy, but without Christ it is meaningless.**]

Acts 4:32-37— [**An equality of needs being met within the body of Christ led to revival.**]

1 Thessalonians 4:11-12— [**We are encouraged to live a quiet, industrious life.**]

P E R S P E C T I V E

2. How do the following factors influence your present spending and lifestyle?

  ▪ Comparing your lifestyle with that of friends and other people —

  ▪ Television, magazines, catalogs, and other advertisements —

  ▪ Your study of the Bible —

  ▪ Your commitment to Christ and to things that are important to Him —

3. Do you sense that the Lord would have you alter any part of your standard of living? If so, what?

REMAINING AGENDA:

1. _____ (5 minutes) **Play the Week 11 segment of the *Practical Application Video* which reviews what the students are required to do for next week.**

  ▪ Read the Perspective Notes on pages 155 to 165 in the *Student Manual.*
  ▪ Complete the Eternity Homework for Week 12 on pages 155 to 165 in the *Student Manual.*
  ▪ Complete the Determining Your Standard of Living on pages 105 to 107 *Practical Application Workbook* and continue budgeting.

2. **Ask your students to be thinking about a "lifetime" or "long-term" prayer request for next week. Also ask them to write a letter to their pastor describing the benefits of the study, because this will encourage the church leadership.**

3. _____ (5 minutes) **Answer any questions concerning the practical applications.**

4. _____ (10 minutes) **Note in the Prayer Logs requests and answers to prayers.**

5. _____ (5 minutes) **End in prayer.**

REMINDER FOR LEADERS: Prepare the Certificates of Achievement for those students who have been faithful.

Leader's Guide for Week 12
ETERNITY

MOSES—
CHOSE ETERNAL RATHER THAN
TEMPORAL VALUES

CROWN'S OVERVIEW OF WEEK 12: This section deals with God's view of our time on earth and eternity. To summarize: life on earth is short and eternity is forever. How we use our time, talents and money will impact eternity.

AGENDA:

1. _____ (5 minutes) **Open in prayer.**

2. _____ (5 minutes) **Everyone individually recites from memory** *Mark 8:36.*

   "For what does it profit a man to gain the whole world, and forfeit his soul?"

3. _____ (5 minutes) **Confirm that everyone has completed the Determining Your Standard of Living practical application, is continuing to budget, and has executed a current will. Answer any questions concerning the practical applications.**

4. _____ (80 minutes) **Begin the group discussion.**

Read the Perspective Notes on pages 155 to 165 and answer:

1. What was the most helpful concept you learned from the notes?

2. Do you sense the Lord would have you alter your lifestyle in any way? If so, in what way?

Read *Psalm 39:4-6* and *Psalm 103:13-16* and answer:

1. What do these passages say to you about the length of life on earth?
   [Life on earth is short.]

Then read *Psalm 90:10, 12*.

2. Why do you think that Moses suggested numbering your days?
   [Numbering our remaining days on earth helps us realize the brevity of our life. Understanding this, we are better able to make wise decisions on how to use our time and money.]

3. Estimate the number of days you have left on earth. How does this impact your thinking?

4. Based on your number of days what actions will you take?

5. In your own words contrast the brevity of life on earth with eternity.

DAY THREE

Read *1 Chronicles 29:15; Philippians 3:20;* **and** *1 Peter 2:11.*

1. What do these passages say about your identity on earth and in heaven?

    1 Chronicles 29:15— [**We are aliens, strangers and sojourners on earth.**]

    Philippians 3:20— [**We are citizens of heaven which is our real home.**]

    1 Peter 2:11— [**We are strangers on this earth.**]

Then read *2 Peter 3:10-13.*

2. In the future what will happen to the earth?
[**The earth and everything on it will be totally destroyed.**]

3. How should this impact the way you invest your time and spend money?

LEADER—you should have approximately **one hour** of class time remaining. We recommend a three-minute stretch break for your group at this time.

Read *Ecclesiates 12:13-14* and *2 Corinthians 5:9-10.*

1. What will happen to each of us in the future?

> *Ecclesiates 12:13-14*— [**The Lord will judge our every deed, even those we think are hidden.**]

> *2 Corinthians 5:9-10*— [**All of us will stand before the judgment-seat of Christ and give an account of our actions.**]

Then read *1 Corinthians 3:11-15.*

2. How would you describe the works (give some examples) that will be burned at this final judgment?

[**Any of our actions done out of what the Bible calls "the flesh"—apart from submission to Christ as Lord. Anything done out of pride or with improper motives.**]

3. Give some examples of works that will be rewarded.

[**The smallest action when done to glorify Christ will be rewarded. In** *Matthew 10:42* **the Lord tells us that even giving someone a cup of cold water shall be rewarded.**]

4. Will all receive the same rewards in heaven?

[**No, some will have done more on earth than others to honor the Lord, and more of their actions will survive judgment and be rewarded.**]

5. What are you doing that will survive this final judgment?

ETERNITY

Read *2 Corinthians 4:18*.

1. What does this verse say to you?

   [**What we see will last only a relatively short period of time. The things we cannot see will last forever and should be of primary importance.**]

2. As you reflect on eternity, answer these questions thoughtfully: What three things do I want to accomplish during the rest of my life?

3. What do I wish to be remembered for?

4. What can I do during my lifetime that would contribute most significantly to the cause of Christ?

5. In light of these answers, what actions or changes do I need to make?

ETERNITY

Read the Eternity Notes on pages 173-180 and answer:

1. What was the most important concept you learned from reading the notes?

2. How will this impact you?

3. Please complete the student Involvement and Suggestions sheet in the *Practical Application Workbook* and send to CROWN. Describe what has been the most beneficial part of the Small Group Study for you:

REMAINING AGENDA:

1. _____ (10 minutes) **Play the Week 12 segment of the *Practical Application Video*.**

2. _____ (5 minutes) **Award the Certificates of Achievement to those who successfully completed the course and collect the student evaluations.**

3. _____ (5 minutes) **Take long-term prayer requests and note them on the Prayer Logs.**

4. _____ (5 minutes) **Leaders pray for each student individually.**

REMINDER FOR LEADERS: We suggest you write each member (or couple) an encouraging letter or e-mail summarizing what you appreciate most about them. May the Lord richly bless you in every way for serving others.

ETERNITY

CROWN wants to obtain your counsel. The suggestions and insights of past participants have significantly improved the study. Please complete and forward this form to CROWN FINANCIAL MINISTRIES, PO Box 100, Gainesville GA 30503-0100. Thank you!

You may complete this form electronically by visiting www.crown.org/lesform.asp.

Please Print

YOUR NAME ☐ MR ☐ MRS ☐ MISS ☐ DR ☐ REV

HOME ADDRESS

CITY   ST/PROV   ZIP/POSTAL CODE

COUNTRY

HOME PHONE   WORK PHONE

CHURCH   CITY   ST/PROV

E-MAIL ADDRESS

3. Describe any insights that would help others.

_____
_____
_____
_____
_____

We would be appreciative if you would share below what the Lord has done in your life through this study, or any practical hints that would be helpful.

4. What the CROWN study has meant to me:

_____
_____
_____
_____
_____
_____
_____
_____
_____
_____
_____
_____
_____
_____

5. Practical Hints:

_____
_____
_____
_____
_____
_____
_____
_____
_____
_____

It is important to track the performance of your students to determine who is faithful. Place your students' names where indicated and place an "x" each week in the appropriate box when they have been faithful in their attendance, scripture memory, practical application, or homework. Leave a box blank if they are not faithful in that particular area. Extra copies of this form may be printed from the CD-ROM in the back of this *Leader's Guide*.

WEEK ENDING	Student Name ▶				
	REQUIREMENTS				
1	ATTENDANCE				
	SCRIPTURE MEMORY				
	PRACTICAL APPLICATION				
	HOMEWORK				
2	ATTENDANCE				
	SCRIPTURE MEMORY				
	PRACTICAL APPLICATION				
	HOMEWORK				
3	ATTENDANCE				
	SCRIPTURE MEMORY				
	PRACTICAL APPLICATION				
	HOMEWORK				
4	ATTENDANCE				
	SCRIPTURE MEMORY				
	PRACTICAL APPLICATION				
	HOMEWORK				
5	ATTENDANCE				
	SCRIPTURE MEMORY				
	PRACTICAL APPLICATION				
	HOMEWORK				
6	ATTENDANCE				
	SCRIPTURE MEMORY				
	PRACTICAL APPLICATION				
	HOMEWORK				

WEEK ENDING				
7				
8				
9				
10				
11				
12				

STUDENT EVALUATION

CARE LOG

Leaders: _____

Beginning Date of Small Group Study: _____

WEEK	Initials of leader responsible for contact ➡	Student(s)	Student(s)	Student(s)	Student(s)	Student(s)	Student(s)
1							
2							
3							
4							
5							
6							
7							
8							
9							
10							
11							
12							

Description of first social activity (conduct about week six):

Description of second social activity (conduct about week twelve):

PRAYER LOG

Be Faithful In Prayer

*"Pray for one another . . . The effective prayer
of a righteous man can accomplish much."*
James 5:16

"Pray for one another." — James 5:16

Name _____   Spouse _____

Home phone _____   Children (ages) _____

Business phone _____   _____

E-mail _____   _____

Home address _____   _____

_____

Week	PRAYER REQUEST(S)	ANSWERS TO PRAYER
1		
2		
3		
4		
5		
6		
7		
8		
9		
10		
11		
12	My long term prayer request:	

PRAYER LOG

"Pray for one another." —JAMES 5:16

Name _____ Spouse _____

Home phone _____ Children (ages) _____

Business phone _____ _____

E-mail _____ _____

Home address _____ _____

_____ _____

WEEK	PRAYER REQUEST(S)	ANSWERS TO PRAYER
1		
2		
3		
4		
5		
6		
7		
8		
9		
10		
11		
12	My long term prayer request:	

"Pray for one another." —JAMES 5:16

Name _____ _____   Spouse _____

Home phone _____   Children (ages) _____

Business phone _____   _____

E-mail _____   _____

Home address _____   _____

_____

Week	Prayer Request(s)	Answers to Prayer
1		
2		
3		
4		
5		
6		
7		
8		
9		
10		
11		
12	My long term prayer request:	

PRAYER LOG

"Pray for one another." — JAMES 5:16

Name _____   Spouse _____

Home phone _____   Children (ages) _____

Business phone _____   _____

E-mail _____   _____

Home address _____   _____

_____   _____

WEEK	PRAYER REQUEST(S)	ANSWERS TO PRAYER
1		
2		
3		
4		
5		
6		
7		
8		
9		
10		
11		
12	My long term prayer request:	

PRAYER LOG

"Pray for one another." —JAMES 5:16

Name _____ Spouse _____

Home phone _____ Children (ages) _____

Business phone _____ _____

E-mail _____ _____

Home address _____ _____

_____ _____

WEEK	PRAYER REQUEST(S)	ANSWERS TO PRAYER
1		
2		
3		
4		
5		
6		
7		
8		
9		
10		
11		
12	My long term prayer request:	

PRAYER LOG

Crown Studies and Helps

Children and Young Adults

This Bible study is full of activities to help make learning basic financial principles fun and exciting. It is designed to be very "hands on" because children this age learn from doing. The **ABC's Leader's Guide** offers the teacher a wide variety of optional activities that reinforce the financial concepts in ways that appeal to young children. Recommended for ages 7 and younger. Can be taught in a small-group setting, a Sunday school class, or one-on-one by a parent.

The ABC's of Handling Money God's Way ....#AB2008 $12.00
(full color, 79 pages, hardcover)

Leader's Guide ....#AL2009 $10.00
(full color, 79 pages, hardcover)

Four children with a financial challenge learn the secret of giving, savings, spending, and much more. They also discover that they can trust God to provide. The principles are embedded in a story of adventure that captures and holds the attention of children. **The Secret** is in a beautifully bound, hardcover Bible study with color illustrations and makes learning about money fun! Recommended for ages 8-12.

The Secret ....#SB2005 $20.00
(full color, 103 pages, hardcover)

The Secret ....#SB2007 $7.00
(black/white, 103 pages, softcover)

The Secret Leader's Guide .....#SL2006 $20.00
(86 pages, softcover)

Teens love this Bible study! Besides memorizing a key Scripture and learning what God says about money, there is also a practical financial exercise at the end of each chapter designed to help teens create habits that will set them on a lifelong journey of handling money responsibly.

Crown Financial Study for Teens Workbook ...#TS2010 $15.00
(180 pages, softcover)

Crown Financial Study for Teens Leaders' Guide #TL2011 $10.00
(86 pages, softcover)

College students are facing growing financial challenges, such as credit card debt and even gambling. The **Crown Collegiate Biblical Financial Study** is an excellent study to teach God's perspective of money to students at the formative time in their lives.

Please call 1-800-722-1976 for more information on how you can administer this study in your own local church or classroom.

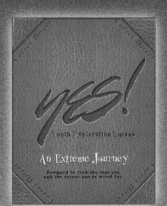

The Career Direct—Youth Exploration Survey® covers four areas: personality, vocational interests, abilities, and priorities. It helps students apply survey results to their current activites and relationships, and it points them toward an exciting future career. YES! is fun, informative, interactive, and biblically based.

Career Direct—YES!® **(guidebook)** ....#CY965 $29.95
(complete package, for individuals or groups)

Career Direct—YES!® **Leaders' Guide** ....#YL187 $14.95
(88 pages, softcover — for youth pastors, guidance counselors, home school leaders)

Measures 12 x 7½ x 2¼ inches

My Giving Bank has been designed to teach your child the value of money and how to handle it in a way that is pleasing to God. When you order this 3-compartment bank made of transparent blue plastic from Crown, we also include free, Bible-based information for parents.

My Giving Bank ....#PK004 $16.95
(for ages 3 and up, includes audio cassette and pamphlet)   Publishers retail price: $19.99

To place your order, contact us at 1-800-722-1976, or visit us online at www.crown.org.

Please note: Prices are subject to change at any time, while supplies last. To check latest prices, call or visit our Web site.

Crown Studies and Helps

Money & Career Management

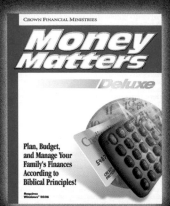

Money Matters Deluxe is Crown's popular budgeting software that brings a fresh view to personal budgeting. It is a total budgeting software package that holds the user accountable by budgeting category. And with enhanced graphics and newer features, **Money Matters Deluxe** makes it even easier to understand the process of managing your personal finances.

Money Matters Deluxe™ . . . . #MD917 $39.95
(CD-ROM format, Windows 95/98/Me)   Publisher's retail price: $49.99

The **Career Direct**® Guidance System on CD-ROM allows you to profile your personality, interests, skills, and work priorities and instantly generates over 30 pages of individualized reports. It also comes with a career-matching feature and a series of audio messages to aid in educational and occupational decision making.

Career Direct® — Educational version #CE950 $89.95
(CD-ROM format, Windows 95/98, for ages 16+)   Publisher's retail price: $106.00

Career Direct® — Occupational version #CO951 $89.95
(CD-ROM format, Windows 95/98, for adults)   Publisher's retail price: $106.00

The **Cash Organizer** envelope budgeting system will simplify your budgeting process. It keeps you in control by tracking the cash portion of your spending.

Twelve Tyvek® envelopes bound in a durable cover with Velcro® closure neatly divide your cash among budget categories. This is the easiest way to begin a controlled spending plan!

Cash Organizer . . . . #CO207 $10.95
(envelope budgeting system, 6¼ x 4 inches) Publisher's retail price: $15.99

The **Budget Counselor Training** course provides focused training for individuals who desire to become volunteer budget counselors. The syllabus contains case studies, counseling procedures and tips, creditinformation, glossary of financial terms, and review questions. This study includes supplemental books and an interactive CD.

Budget Counselor Training course . . . . #SS208 $125.00
(self-study course)   Publisher's retail price: $125.00

With the **Bill Organizer**, there's no more searching frantically for that misplaced phone bill or wondering if the power bill has been paid! This expanding file of durable green transparent plastic contains 12 tabbed pockets that can be customized easily to organize your bills by either category or due date!

Preprinted stickers and ledger sheets for tracking your payments are included.

Also included with your **Bill Organizer** purchase is the helpful audio tape, "Taking Charge of Your Credit Card."

Bill Organizer . . . . #BO905 $10.95
(10¼ x 5½ inches)   Publisher's retail price: $15.99

Please note: Prices are subject to change at any time, while supplies last. To check latest prices, call or visit our Web site.

For a complete listing of products and services available from Crown Financial Ministries, contact us for a free catalog at 1-800-722-1976 or visit us online at www.crown.org.